Inspired To WIN

7 Strategies To Help You Stand Out
And
WIN In Any Organization.

Introduction

Congratulations!

Since you are reading this book, I presume there is something in your personal and professional life that you are looking to change or transform into something greater. It shows that you are willing to learn and try something different to see different results. There's a quote that says, "Insanity is doing the same thing over and over again and expecting different results." I believe that you have passed that stage and are ready to do something different to experience something different.

This book is going to help you transform your life if you implement the strategies, principles, and lessons being taught. This book will be your help guide to create a better professional and personal life. If you are looking to WIN, then I encourage you to use and adopt the information presented here to help you do just that, WIN.

There are 7 key strategies that will be shared in this book that you can use not just in any organization, but in any setting. These strategies are principles that never change. Each one builds on the other, you just need to be ready to start building.

.... Now let's begin with the 7 strategies that will be discussed in this book to help you WIN and keep WINNING!

Chapter One:

Winning With Confidence

Confidence is a word we often hear a lot, but contrary to what you may believe about the overuse of the expression, it is a valid and needed word for anyone that is looking to do greater things in life. Confidence give you the courage to move forward when fear is in your ear telling you that you cannot do something that you so desperately desire to do. It provides you with the power you need to step out and try something anyway whether you win or lose.

Along with confidence comes the right attitude. When you are determined to have a positive outlook on life, your career, and every other area of your life, this feeds your confidence muscle and gives you the courage and strength to become who you were created to be. So many times, people don't move forward in life or in their job, simply because they doubt themselves and feel as though they are not enough or don't have enough education to move to the next level that they desire.

This is called fear. Fear stifles your ability to move forward with your dreams, hopes, and desires. Fear keeps you stagnant and sometimes running in circles where you are most comfortable. I want to help you understand that whatever it is you desire for your life; you can accomplish it!

All it takes is for you to build your confidence muscle little by little, which may mean doing something small every day, week, or month to achieve your desired results. I encourage you to try something you've never tried before, but always wished you could.

In your job, if there is an ideal role that you see yourself doing, find out how to get there and start the journey of preparation to get there. This may mean going back to school, taking additional certification classes, and meeting people who are connected to that ideal role who may be able to open the door for you.

You have the power within to change everything about yourself and your life to get where you really desire to be. I have had many different careers over the span of my early life, but this just shows I was willing to try something different and become something more at each stage of my life.

At age 21, I opened my own Spa and operated that business for over 10 years. I was young, but I wasn't afraid to try. Not long after that, I started a real estate investment firm, where again I new nothing about the business, but took it upon myself to learn and meet new people who could teach me what I didn't know. I learned how to buy dilapidated properties and flip them for a profit for little or no money out of pocket.

Then I decided I wanted to start a fashion brand, again no background in fashion, but saw a need a created a handbag on wheels and received a patent on it, even when I was told it wasn't possible. After that, I said I wanted to see what it was like to work in corporate America and for 10 years I worked in medical sales and achieved substantial incentive awards.

My second year in the company I won an all expense trip for me and my spouse to Hawaii. Sometimes I pinch myself for all the opportunities that I have had and the successes that I was able to experience all because I wasn't afraid to try something different that interest me.

Now, I have the most amazing opportunity where I can use all my experiences, wisdom, and knowledge to teach others how to win with my training consulting firm. All you need to do is put fear behind you and build your confidence in small steps and you too can accomplish anything.

This may require you to talk to yourself sometimes and speak positive affirmations over your life. I love affirmations, everyday they help me move into my greatness. I recommend that you too use affirmations everyday to help build your confidence muscle and you can start here.

Please use the list below to begin your positive affirmation journey and there is space left for you to write in your own if you so desire.

Confidence Affirmations

I am courageous. I am willing to act in spite of any fear.

It's easy to make friends. I attract positive and kind people into my life.

It's easy to meet people. I create positive and supportive relationships.

I AM a powerful creator. I create the life I want.

I AM wonderful as I am. I accept and love myself.

I AM confident. I trust myself.

I AM successful right now.

I AM passionate. I AM outrageously enthusiastic and inspire others.

I have unlimited power at my disposal.

I AM optimistic. I believe things will always work out for my good.

I AM____

I AM____

I AM____

I AM____

I AM____

I AM____

I AM____

I AM____

I AM____

I AM____

Chapter Two:

Finding Your Voice

The power of your voice! How do you find the power of your voice? This is the next strategy that is going to help you win in any organization and setting. We all were created with a unique voice print that cannot be duplicated. From the sound, to the pitch, and what come out from your mind. No two people on this planet are alike and your voice will definitely take you places if you let it.

I always hear people say I am afraid to speak in public or I don't like to speak in public. The fact is, this is the number one fear in the world, but it doesn't have to be your fear. Your voice and speaking ability have the power to open so many doors for you if you only give yourself permission to do it.

There hasn't been a single thing in this world that has been created without someone sharing information about it. Every cause needs a voice and every voice has an audience.

Although this may be area that you shy away from, it is the best free tool that you can use to create opportunities for your career and life. Like anything you do, it takes practice and work to be successful at it.

I always share that the best place to start is to find an elementary school where you can go and read to the students, because these little ones will be your best audience. They will praise you, they won't hear your mistakes, and they will help build your confidence to get you to the next audience.

The other advice I give is to join your local Toastmaster's group. This group is strictly created to help you learn the craft. They will count all your ums and ahs and critique you to no end, but it is a learning environment created to help build your ability to speak and help you overcome your fear of speaking.

Also, while you are there make sure you participate in their local, regional, state, and national speaking competitions. This is where the excitement comes in, but again you are building your speaking muscle and the power of your voice.

Personally, I enjoyed Toastmasters, the opportunity to compete against other speakers helped me hone my craft to become a better speaker. I had the privilege of winning local and regional contests and even met some of the world champion speakers that came from Toastmasters.

It is an awesome experience if you want to take it that far. But beyond that, your voice is needed in your community to help create change for causes like human sex trafficking, domestic violence, or any other cause that pulls on your heartstrings. Your voice is needed in your workplace to help create change, to improve processes, to help mentor, and elevate others. When you understand how powerful your voice is, then you will also understand that your voice will create new opportunities for you to advance your life and career.

The world needs to hear your voice and there are people who are assigned to you that you haven't even met and won't meet until you show up with the power of your voice to help change their life.

From this day forward, I want to encourage you to use your voice every chance you get, even if it is volunteer to lead a meeting or a webinar, you have to start somewhere if you want to continue to grow and develop yourself.

You can do this, remember in chapter one, all you need is your confidence to get your there. I am cheering for you because I believe in you!

Please use the list below to begin your positive affirmation journey and there is space left for you to write in your own if you so desire.

Speaking Affirmations

I Am a confident public speaker.

I Am relaxed when speaking publicly.

I Am at my best when speaking to a large crowd.

I AM excited and positive when giving a public speech.

I AM a naturally calm public speaker.

I AM a great public speaker.

I always speak calmly and clearly.

I AM fearless when speaking to large crowds.

I AM a successful public speaker.

Others admire my ability to speak publicly.

*I AM*____

*I AM*____

*I AM*____

*I AM*____

*I AM*____

*I AM*____

*I AM*____

*I AM*____

*I AM*____

Chapter Three:

Dressing To WIN

I thought it would be important to have this topic as a strategy to win, simply because society have changed so much over the years and have lost many of the standards that use to be in place as it relates to image. It amazes me that people don't consider this strategy to be important and it is not being taught in schools to help our young people as they go out looking for jobs and careers after college.

Dressing for the role that you desire carries lots of weight, whether you realize its importance or not. From the moment you meet someone, within 3-5 seconds they have already determined if they are attracted to you, like you, or want to do business with you.

First impressions are lasting, whether you are applying to grad school, interviewing for a job, or attending a networking event. People are sizing you up and how you dress plays a very important role. You can choose to dress for success or for failure. You may feel that just because your office doesn't have a dress code or policy, it is ok to go to work with stretch pants, flipflops, wrinkled clothes, and short skirts so short that if you bend over too far everything shows and no one will bother you. The question is, what is your mindset for your attire. What are you thinking or feeling about yourself? Have you ever thought what people may be thinking of you? Whether what they are thinking of you is true or false, it doesn't matter, because that is the impression you gave them based on your outer appearance.

In an article, in Forbes magazine written by Brandon Vallorani, he quotes Thomas Edison, "Opportunity is missed by most people because it was dressed in overalls and looks like work." The author continues by saying that this happens every day: people who have great talent and potential are overlooked for growth opportunities because they don't look, smell, or sound like a million bucks. Coco Channel, the founder of Chanel, once said, "Dress shabbily and they remember the dress: dress impeccably and they remember the woman."

Bottom line if you want to be recognized as already successful or competent for the new opportunity you are seeking, you have to look the part every day. There should never be a dress down day. When you walk out of your door you should have the mindset that I am meeting my next opportunity today.

You never know who you will meet in the grocery store or at the stoplight and what opportunity you will miss because you didn't look your best. According to the Forbes article, Dressing for Success and The Achievement of Your Dream, the author shares a recent study that shows that people who dress better have more confidence, feel more powerful, and are more focused on details. Vallaroni also shares that people perceive well dressed people as leaders and go to them for support at a faster rate than those not as well dressed. He also shares a quote by Academy Award Winner Edith Head, which says, "You can have anything you want in life if you dress for it." This statement is powerful, it simply means that whatever you desire in and for your life start by dressing for the part.

There is a dress code everywhere and it may be invisible, but even if you work in a cubicle on the phones, someone is watching you and most definitely someone is hearing you on the other end and it is your dress and appearance that will give you the needed confidence to speak to the person on the phone and persuade them to act on your request.

Your next promotion also plays a part in how you are seen in your cubicle every day. Leaders know how to spot leaders.

So, if you are ready to WIN big use this strategy to get you closer to your goal.

Please use the list below to begin your positive affirmation journey and there is space left for you to write in your own if you so desire.

Dressing/Image Affirmations

Everything I wear says beauty, freedom, health, prosperity, and happiness.

I act with assurance, confidence and grace.

I always ensure that I look my best.

I always give a fantastic first impression.

I always look and dress the part I wish to portray.

I always look smart and fashionable and successful.

I always present myself in my best light.

I AM chic and sophisticated.

I AM a sharp dresser.

I AM beauty and strength combined.

*I AM*_______________________________________

*I AM*_____________________________________

*I AM*______________________________________

*I AM*____

*I AM*______________________________________

*I AM*____

*I AM*____

*I AM*_______________________________________

*I AM*____

Chapter Four:

Managing Your Time To WIN

Time management and managing priorities are courses that are requested of me to teach often in small and large organizations. The fact is we all need order and need to learn how to manage our time well to be successful. Everyday we are pulled in so many directions, not only do we have demands from home, work, and or school; we have demands from our social life on Facebook, Instagram, and Twitter. We have become consumed with busyness and time wasters that we sometime lose sight on our goals and what is really important for our lives.

What I know is that managing multiple projects, objectives, and deadlines can be a full-time job in itself. Because of this, it requires your full attention, concentration, skills, talents, and dedication. If you want to be successful in this area you must identify your challenges and gain control of your life.

I would encourage you to begin by compartmentalizing each area of your life and then create a priority list for the projects and deadlines within that category.

For example: home, school, work, church, or any other outside activity that you may be apart of. Create a category for each and then identify what's most important in each category.

After you have created your categories, the first step is to mentally prepare and focus on your list of things that are important.

Secondly, set goals. Without them, you don't know where you are going, how to get there, or if you have arrived.

Thirdly, Focus on one or two tasks at a time. Focusing on more than this can lead to frustration and incomplete work.

Fourthly, identify your challenges and work to overcome them, be committed to learning new skills, gaining new knowledge, and increasing your abilities.

Lastly, make the most of your unscheduled time. Be sure to always allow time for yourself. This will reduce stress and increase your productivity.

Here are some addition strategies that can help you WIN as you begin to manage your time:

1. Break your project down into smaller components. *For example:* This morning, I will spend 20 minutes doing task number 1. This afternoon, I will spend 15 minutes doing task number 2 and so on.
2. Do the task you dread the most first. *For example:* You may hate going through two weeks of accumulated email, but you do it first and in small increments to get it done.

3. Promise to reward yourself with each increment of organization accomplished. *For example:* As soon as I get these emails answered, I will go to lunch, or I will go get my nails done. Anything that you deem will be rewarding to you.
4. Before meetings, determine your desired results. Have a clear purpose in mind before starting the meeting. Your team will waste less time by getting back to work as soon as you meet your agenda.
5. Plan your week on Sunday. Breakdown your weekly goals into daily tasks, so you only need to glance at your list while working. Walking into work with a plan for the week will help you focus on your priorities. You can easily transition from your weekend mindset to your productive Monday morning mindset.
6. Don't wait for inspiration- do it now. With mindfulness, you don't have to feel like getting

something done to do it. Notice the thoughts and feelings that will arise while you work from an outside perspective. You don't need the perfect environment to start your task.

7. Learn to say NO. Your time is precious, and you don't have the time to waste it on people and projects that don't align with your mission and goals.

This strategy will help you WIN in every area of your life if you begin to implement the tools provided above.

Please use the list o to bn the next page to begin your positive affirmation journey and there is space left for you to write in your own if you so desire.

Time Management Affirmations

I give myself time to do each task at perfect speed.

I have a great respect for other people's time.

I have absolute control over my time.

I have all the time I need to accomplish all that I want to do.

I have complete freedom over how I use my time.

I create prioritized to-do lists and follow them through.

I have lots of free time in which to create my perfect life.

I have plenty of time to do the things I want to do.

I have plenty of time to improve my life.

I have the power to complete everything I want to do today.

I AM____

I AM____

I AM____

I AM____

I AM____

I AM____

I AM____

I AM____

I AM____

I AM____

Chapter Five:

Being Assertive To WIN

What does it really mean to be assertive? Many people use this term loosely and others take assertiveness to the extreme by using aggression. The truth is that it is very important to understand how to use your assertiveness skills not only in the workplace, but even at home when communicating with your family.

Assertiveness is NOT aggression nor is it being passive or passive-aggressive. Being assertive simply means standing up for yourself when you need to. Most women have the most difficult time in this area for fear of believing they will hurt someone else's feelings. They usually want to avoid confrontation and confusion.

On the other hand, you have some people who are extremely confrontational, who get angry easily, and can sometimes be violent which can cause even more trouble. Both types need to know how to be assertive.

Assertiveness is about expressing your needs while respecting the other person (but not fear) for the other person and his/her point of view, but also standing up for your own point of view. The great thing about assertiveness is that once you master it, it will improve your communication with your friends, family, children, and business associates.

Here are examples adopted fromwww.infocounseling.com:

So, you've been asked to take out the garbage and you don't want to do it. Here are the possible responses:

Aggressive: "I am not taking out the stinking garbage! I always do it and you can do it yourself!"

Passive: "Ok. I'll take out the garbage."

Passive-Aggressive: Either saying you will take it out and then not doing it. Or saying you will take it out and then adding a sarcastic remark, "Is there anything else I can do for you while I am at it?"

Assertive: "Actually, I took out the garbage the last few times. I am thinking that it is someone else's turn to take the garbage out this time!"

How may times have you taken the passive or passive-aggressive stance? These two are probably the easiest routes to take if you are non-confrontational person.

One of the best tools you can use when you begin practicing your assertiveness skills is the pronoun "**I**". This can help you say NO without using the word NO. "I" statements help you share your thoughts, feelings, wants, and opinions in a clear precise and respectful way without blaming.

The goal is to keep the focus on the problem and not the person.

Here are some examples adopted from www.blog.learnit.com:

"I'd like to be able to give my opinion without interruption" is much more effective than, "You're always interrupting me".

"I get angry when he breaks promises," instead of, "He makes me angry."

"I believe the best policy is to..." instead of, "The only sensible thing to do is..."

"The punctuation could be better, and the formatting is inconsistent", is less threatening

"Will you please....?" is more effective than one that asks, "Would you mind..." – or even worse, the request that demands, "Why don't you...?

Please use the list on the next page to begin your positive affirmation journey and there is space left for you to write in your own if you so desire.

Assertiveness Affirmations

I AM assertive.

I speak my mind at the right time.

I tell others how I feel immediately.

I stand up for myself all the time.

I AM confident when talking to others.

I AM firm with others when needed.

I set boundaries and tell others what I want.

I speak my mind openly without fear.

I confidently take control of a situation when needed.

I express myself honestly.

*I AM*____

*I AM*____

*I AM*____

*I AM*____

*I AM*____

*I AM*____

*I AM*____

*I AM*____

*I AM*____

*I AM*____

Chapter Six:

Negotiating To WIN

Negotiation skills is a strategy that can be used not only in business, but with your family and friends. These skills should only focus on the facts to help you persuade others to give you what you want and to give the other person what they want. The goal is to create a win-win solution where both parties get what they want without sacrificing their objectives.

You may need to do your research and prepare prior to the negotiation so that you are well informed with what the other person is looking for. To be effective at negotiating, you begin by preparing for the negotiation, then use the WIIFT (What's In It For Them) approach, your goal is to aim high- set your price high, so you have room to make concessions later if necessary.

Your next strategy is to use your communication skills to build and maintain solid relationships. You do this by keeping your word and being a great person to do business with.

Finally, it is important that you are honest and ethical. You may ask what can be negotiated, the answer is simply, everything.

Anything that has value can be negotiated. Many people think of negotiation only when it comes to asking for a raise or for a certain salary requests when applying for a job. This will be a good place to start.

When you are preparing to negotiate your salary, the first order of business is to research, research, and research. You have to know the industry standards for the job you are currently in or the one you are looking to obtain. If you can't find it on any of the job sites, start talking to people who are in similar positions or who have held supervisory roles that would be willing to share.

Once you have gathered this information, make sure you have a low, mid, and high-end range so you have room to negotiate from the top. Money may not be your motivator and if that is the case evaluate what else will bring value to you that can be negotiated, such as flex time, extra vacation time, or working remotely.

As you negotiate what you want, remember your worth, the value you bring to the organization, and how you can create a win-win solution for you and the organization. Women sometimes feel that they have to justify why they are deserving of a raise and will sometimes share too much of their personal information during the negotiation for the pay raise and this is absolutely unnecessary. Stick to the facts of your job performance and your past merits only.

This is how you sell your value. Negotiation skills can play an important role in your growth and development. Remember if you refuse to ask or speak up for what you know you are worth you are closing yourself off to the opportunity to have the things you desire most. I encourage you to give it a try. Afterall what is there to lose.

Please use the list on the next page to begin your positive affirmation journey and there is space left for you to write in your own if you so desire.

Negotiation Affirmations

I AM a great negotiator.

I AM constantly creating win-win solutions.

I AM creating negotiation deals that benefit me and my family.

I AM meeting great people who are willing to collaborate with me.

I AM a magnet for great negotiation deals.

I AM forming new relationship with the people I am negotiating with.

I AM making decisions that create positive relationships.

I AM prepared with the best negotiation strategy I can offer.

I AM asking the right questions to get me closer to closing the deal in my favor.

I AM carefully evaluating all opportunities that are presented to me.

I AM_____________________________________

I AM_____________________________________

I AM_____________________________________

I AM_____________________________________

I AM_____________________________________

I AM_____________________________________

I AM_____________________________________

I AM_____________________________________

I AM_____________________________________

I AM_____________________________________

Chapter Seven:

Selling To WIN

Sales is a word that most people shy away from. They say things like, "I don't like selling." Or "I'm not a salesperson." What a myth. We are all salespeople whether we think so or not. Everything you do involves selling. You sell yourself everyday when you meet people, go for an interview, or develop new relationships.

Beyond this concept, there is the hard or consultative sales role that does exist. Even if you have this title, you must remember that people don't buy because you have the best widget. They buy because they like you first, you are fulfilling a need or gap, and or there is a benefit to them of what you are selling.

Number one, is they like you, because if they don't like or trust you, they will never buy from you.

People do hate being sold to, but if you work toward building trust by learning something about them before you present your sales pitch you will have an opportunity to develop a relationship to make it easier to make the sale later.

In building this relationship, you must nurture it over time. When you are identifying your potential buyer, you need to use a measurable and repeatable sales process, know your product inside and out, believe in what you are selling, always follow up, and finally, don't be afraid of rejection.

You will hear the word No, but don't let that discourage you and make you quit. I always remembered Les Brown say, "Make No Your Vitamin." If you quit too early, you will never reach your yes and remember for every no, there is a yes waiting on you.

In my early 20s when I started my first company, I had to learn how to sell myself. I was selling massages and spa services to people who had never heard of me. I had no background in business or sales, but I had a passion for what I was doing, and I knew I could help heal and make people feel better.

One evening, I attended my local Chamber of Commerce meeting with a stack of business cards in my hand. Before stepping out of my car, I gave myself a pep talk and told myself that I was not allowed to leave the event until I introduced myself and business and passed out every card I had brought with me.

Talk about being scared, I was very nervous, but I had made a deal with myself that I could not break. That night, I passed out all of my cards and met so many new people and that was the beginning of the success of my new business.

Sometimes, you just have to step outside of our comfort zone and do something you've never done before. I encourage you to take risk everyday to become a better version of yourself.

Sales doesn't have to be dreadful if you love what you are selling. When you love what you are selling, the people you are selling to will feel your energy and be compelled to purchase what you have to offer. Remember, they must like you first.

Please use the list on the next page to begin your positive affirmation journey and there is space left for you to write in your own if you so desire.

Selling Affirmations

I AM a skilled salesperson.

I AM knowledgeable about the products I sell.

I AM persuasive and convincing.

I AM a great communicator.

I AM focused on developing my sales skills.

I have a product/service that everyone wants.

I instinctively know how to get someone to buy.

I AM in tune with my customer's needs.

I AM committed to becoming a highly successful salesperson.

I AM able to turn any transaction into one that is mutually beneficial.

*I AM*____

*I AM*____

*I AM*____

*I AM*____

*I AM*____

*I AM*____

*I AM*____

*I AM*____

*I AM*____

*I AM*____

About the Author

TIFFANY ANISETTE PRINGLE is married to O.C Pringle, VP of Inspire CMG and the mother of 3 beautiful children, Taevondru Emanuel White (19), Jaelen Esais White (18), and Vashti Propheci Pringle (4). She is a **U.S Patent Recipient, Author, Speaker, Corporate Trainer, and Coach.** She is a highly motivated Corporate Trainer and Facilitator with experience in training small and large groups across diverse industries. Proven success in leveraging education and experiences to deliver successful training programs onsite and virtually.

With over 15 years of entrepreneurship and corporate sales experience, Tiffany is a successful leader, facilitator, motivator, and coach with a passion for creating high performance teams, training other trainers, and developing leaders at all levels of an organization. Tiffany is the Founder of Inspire Consulting & Management Group and the former Chair of The African American Leadership Council for Field and Sales Engagement Team for Baxter Healthcare.

As a sought-out speaker, Tiffany has been the keynote presenter and workshop facilitator for corporations such as Verizon Wireless, Georgia Power, WOW, Delta Airlines, Hospitals, Gwinnett County, Polk County, White County, Atlanta Metro University, University of Athens, Beaufort County School System, Blue Cross Blue Shield, Humana, Employee Assistance Programs (EAP Work Life Program) and Non-Profit organizations. Workshop and Training subjects included: Time Management, Organization Management, Increasing Morale, The Power of Positive Thinking, Diversity in the Workplace, Effective Communication, Presentation Skills, Leadership Skills, and other Personal and Professional Development Trainings.

Beyond her expertise in corporate settings, Tiffany has founded a number of companies and is a recipient of a Patent from the US Patent Trade Office on her innovative Handbag on Wheels. She also creates motivational self-help books and products for the empowerment of women and young girls. The first book titled, "Dare To Be A Diamond", has since become a non-profit organization called "The Diamond Movement" where young girls and women can go to be empowered and inspired. She continues to speak and provide workshops and trainings on the subjects of entrepreneurship and empowerment throughout the country.

To schedule Tiffany Anisette Pringle or her team to speak at your

next event contact 404-308-5868 or tiffanyconsults@gmail.com

Made in the USA
Columbia, SC
13 May 2022

60367935R00028